# TURTLE

## PETS WE LOVE

Lynn Hamilton and Katie Gillespie

www.av2books.com

## Step 1
Go to **www.av2books.com**

## Step 2
Enter this unique code

**URGJE629D**

## Step 3
Explore your interactive eBook!

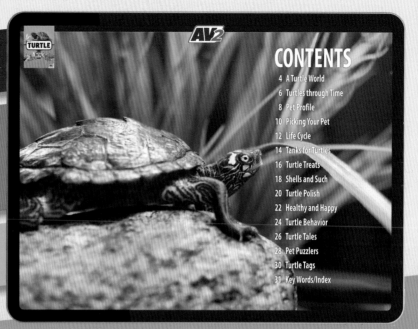

### CONTENTS

**AV2 is optimized for use on any device**

# Your interactive eBook comes with...

**Contents**
Browse a live contents page to easily navigate through resources

**Audio**
Listen to sections of the book read aloud

**Videos**
Watch informative video clips

**Weblinks**
Gain additional information for research

**Try This!**
Complete activities and hands-on experiments

**Key Words**
Study vocabulary, and complete a matching word activity

**Quizzes**
Test your knowledge

**Slideshows**
View images and captions

# ... and much, much more!

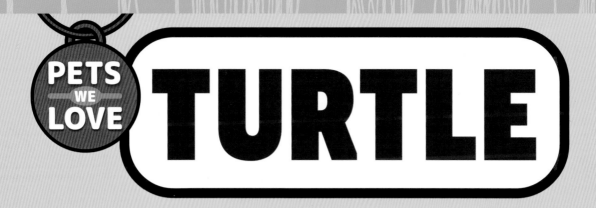

# PETS WE LOVE TURTLE

# Contents

# A Turtle World

There are many different kinds of turtles, each with their own names. Turtles that live on land are called tortoises. Freshwater turtles are called aquatic, or water, turtles. Turtles that live in the ocean are known as sea turtles. These interesting animals have fascinated people for hundreds of years.

Turtles are most easily recognized for the shells they carry on their backs. They are also well known for moving slowly on land. Even though they do not bark, purr, or cuddle like some animals, turtles make rewarding pets. Each turtle has a personality and routine all her own. Keeping a turtle as a pet is a unique way to welcome a piece of nature into your life.

Turtles are popular pets in the United States. More than 13 percent of homes have a specialty pet, which includes turtles.

There are about **300** known species of turtles.

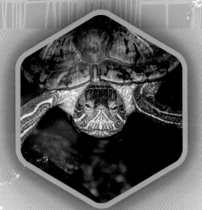

Some turtles may grow until age **50**.

The biggest turtle ever measured was about **9 feet** in length. (3 meters)

Turtle shells have between **59** and **61** bones.

The oldest evidence of ancient turtles was found in China.

A turtle's **shell** has **two** parts called the **carapace** (top) and the **plastron** (bottom).

The **oldest** recorded turtle lived to be **188** years old.

A turtle from **60 million** years ago was the size of a small **car**.

# Turtles through Time

Turtles are a fascinating link to the past. The first turtles lived about 220 million years ago. They shared Earth with dinosaurs. We can learn about these turtles from their **fossils**. Today's turtles have many of the same qualities as their ancestors. However, there are some significant differences. Unlike present-day turtles, ancient turtles had teeth. They also had spiny armor covering their tails and necks and were unable to pull their necks inside their shells.

Over time, turtles have changed to suit their environments. Land turtles have strong, thick shells. These shells help to protect them from dangerous **predators**. Sea turtles are strong swimmers, thanks to their flat shells and paddle-like legs.

Turtles belong to a group called reptiles. This means they have lungs, scales, and lay their eggs on land. Reptiles are also cold-blooded. Other animals belonging to this group include lizards, snakes, alligators, and crocodiles.

Turtles have been connected to people for a very long time. These animals were once used for food during long trips across the ocean. People have made turtle shells into jewelry. Some Native American creation stories even feature turtles.

# Pet Profile

There are many kinds of turtles. Each has different needs. To live long, happy lives, pet turtles must be cared for properly. Some turtles are mainly land animals, while others are more often found in the water. Most turtles spend their time both on land and in water. It is important to provide your pet turtle with a tank that suits him. Turtles that **hibernate** will need a place to do so safely. Your pet will also require regular grooming, feeding, and visits to the **veterinarian**.

## Red-Eared Sliders
- Can live for more than 25 years
- Are active during the day
- Grow about 11 or 12 inches (28 or 30 centimeters) long
- Have olive-green skin with yellow markings
- Have red patches near the ears
- Like to swim but need dry land as well
- May be aggressive toward people or other turtles

## Spotted Turtles
- Are mostly **carnivorous**
- Grow about 5 inches (13 cm) long
- Have a black carapace with orange spots
- Have brown eyes if male and yellow eyes if female
- Like to swim
- May be aggressive toward other turtles

## Wood Turtles

- Can live for at least 25 years
- Grow about 10 inches (25 cm) long
- Have **scutes** in the shape of four-sided peaks
- Enjoy climbing and digging
- May learn to recognize their owner
- Need both land and water areas in their tank

## Painted Turtles

- Can live for about 20 years
- Are active during the day
- Grow about 8 to 10 inches (20 to 25 cm) long
- Have some red markings on their carapace and legs
- Have yellow markings on their head
- Need an aquarium with a **basking** surface

## Musk Turtles

- Are mostly carnivorous
- Grow up to 5 inches (13 cm) long
- Can climb well
- Spray a smelly liquid when upset
- May be aggressive toward other turtles
- Are closely related to mud turtles

## Box Turtles

- Eat both meat and plants
- Can live between 30 and 40 years
- Grow about 6 to 8 inches (15 to 20 cm) long
- Have a black or brown carapace with yellow, brown, and orange markings
- Are able to tuck their arms and legs inside their hinged shell

Red-eared sliders are one of the most popular turtle pets.

Some turtles **dive** up to **3,000** feet below the ocean surface. (914 m)

The **fastest** turtles can swim up to **22** miles per hour. (35 kilometers)

Galapagos tortoises travel about **18** times **slower** than people.

# Picking Your Pet

Caring for a pet turtle is a big responsibility. Owners must be familiar with turtle behavior. They also have to recreate their pet's natural environment. It is important to know that turtles will hide in their shells if they are scared. They can also be active animals that are fun to watch.

## Can I Provide a Suitable Home for a Turtle?

If the climate is suitable, your pet turtle may spend some time outside. However, it is not safe to release your pet into nature. The local environment may not fit her needs.

The safest place for your turtle is inside her tank, whether it is an indoor aquarium or an outdoor enclosure. The temperature should be carefully controlled. Make sure that the tank is placed on a sturdy surface away from potential dangers. Keep your turtle protected from other pets.

## What Will a Turtle Cost?

Some turtles are quite affordable. However, it can be expensive to set up your pet's tank. Other costs include food, cleaning products, and tank supplies. She will also require yearly visits to the veterinarian.

## Am I Ready to Care for a Turtle?

Before deciding to become a turtle owner, make sure you have time in your schedule to spend with your pet. You will need to care for her every day. A routine will be very important. If you are away from home, someone reliable will need to look after your turtle.

# Life Cycle

Some turtles are born and raised in captivity. Others are collected from nature and sold as pets. Your turtle will have different needs throughout his life. Learning more about each stage of your turtle's development will help you provide him with the best possible care.

## Eggs

Female turtles dig a hole to lay their eggs inside. They cover the eggs with plant matter and soil to keep them warm and protected. Depending on their species, turtles lay anywhere from a few eggs to hundreds of eggs. They take about two to three months to hatch. Turtle breeders may place eggs inside an **incubator**. This keeps them safe from the cold and from predators.

## Growth and Maturity

Turtles have growth rings on their shells. Growth rings provide information about his growing stages. At age 3, turtles are about one-third of their adult size. By age 6, they are two-thirds grown. A turtle's life span depends on many factors. His species, environment, and the quality of the care he receives will all impact how long a turtle lives.

## Hatchlings

Hatchlings break out of their eggs using a sharp point on the tip of their beak-like jaw. This is called an egg tooth. It falls off once the turtle has hatched. The hatching process can take minutes, hours, or even a few days. Baby turtles must dig up to reach the surface.

## Baby Turtles

Baby turtles have a special yolk sac attached to their plastron. They feed off this for about one week after birth. The yolk sac detaches from their body when it is no longer needed. Baby turtles need special nutrition to help their shells properly develop.

The amount of water in a turtle's tank depends on the animal's size. For every 1 inch (2.5 cm) of length, there should be about 10 gallons (38 liters) of water.

# Tanks for Turtles

Some turtles may be kept outside during the warm months of summer. If you keep your pet turtle outdoors, she will need an enclosure covered in wire mesh. This will help protect her from outdoor predators. If you keep your pet indoors, an aquarium or sturdy plastic container are options.

Cover the bottom of your turtle's tank in gravel or artificial grass. You can find these materials at a pet store. Choose the materials you place in your turtle's home carefully. Some may be difficult to keep clean. Others may be small enough for her to swallow, which can be dangerous. Find out if your turtle needs a place to dig and burrow. Some species like to have places to hide. You can put a hollowed log or a wooden box in your turtle's tank for this purpose.

Turtles have very specific needs. They require sunlight or lighting with ultraviolet B rays to stay healthy. The lighting in your turtle's tank should match the natural changes in sunlight. Make sure your pet has a water container for swimming or wading and a dry surface for basking. She will need a ramp to climb out of the water. Put a heating light above one end of her basking area.

Thermometers can help you to regulate the temperature in your turtle's tank. A special heater will keep the water warm, and a filter will keep it clean. Place a cover over your pet's enclosure as well. This will keep her safe from other family pets or small children.

Young turtles must be fed every day. Older turtles only need feeding around three times a week.

# Turtle Treats

Turtles can be picky about their food. Since it is important for your pet to eat a healthy mix of foods, you should cut his meals up into small pieces. This will stop him from picking out his favorite foods and ensure he gets a varied diet. Include fruits and vegetables, such as blueberries, cantaloupes, carrots, peas, and cucumbers, in your pet's meals. Always wash these kinds of foods before feeding them to your turtle.

Some turtles prefer more meat in their diet. You can give your turtle foods such as insects, snails, crayfish, trout, and freshwater shrimp. Turtles also need calcium in their diet. Calcium helps keep their bones and shells healthy. You can find calcium, vitamin, and other mineral **supplements** at pet stores.

Your pet turtle may overeat. Watch for signs that he is overweight. These include a bulging tail, underside, and legs. To make sure that your turtle stays healthy, talk to your veterinarian. She can suggest the right foods for your pet as well as a suitable feeding schedule. It is also best to separate land and water turtles during feeding times. This will keep them from biting one another when reaching for food.

# Shells and Such

Turtles have many traits that are well suited to their particular way of life. Knowing more about your turtle's physical features will help you improve your skills as a pet owner. Understanding how your pet's body works and **adapts** to the world around her will allow you to create a suitable home to meet her needs.

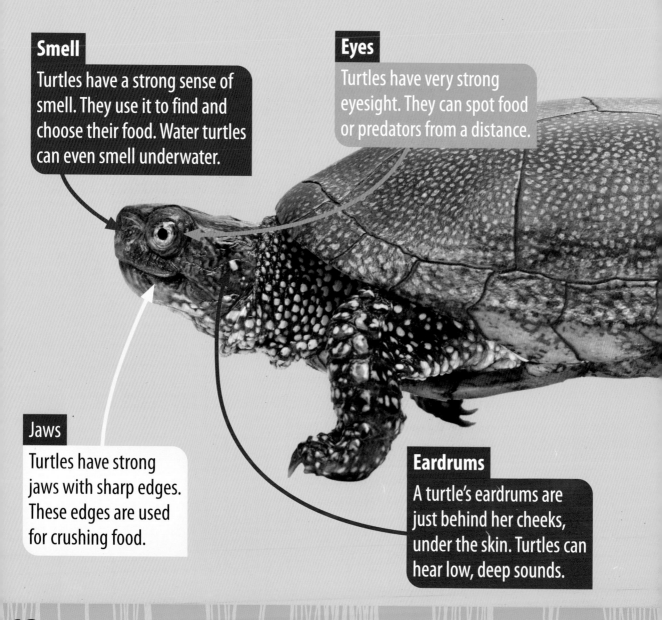

**Smell**
Turtles have a strong sense of smell. They use it to find and choose their food. Water turtles can even smell underwater.

**Eyes**
Turtles have very strong eyesight. They can spot food or predators from a distance.

**Jaws**
Turtles have strong jaws with sharp edges. These edges are used for crushing food.

**Eardrums**
A turtle's eardrums are just behind her cheeks, under the skin. Turtles can hear low, deep sounds.

**Shell**

A turtle's carapace is joined to her plastron by bony bridges. The surface of her shell is made of **keratin**.

**Tail**

One way to tell male and female turtles apart is by their tails. Generally, males have thicker, longer, and more pointed tails than females.

**Skin**

Turtles have scales all over their skin. These scales help prevent moisture loss.

You should never paint your pet turtle's shell. This can be very dangerous to his health.

# Turtle Polish

It is essential to keep your pet turtle's home clean. One way to reduce mess is to feed your turtle in a small, separate container or tank. This will help to keep his main tank clean. It is important to remove any uneaten food or waste on a regular basis.

The water in your pet's aquarium must be changed often as well. Placing a filter in the tank helps to keep the water clean. If you are using a filter, you will not have to change the water as frequently. Be sure to check and clean the filter when needed.

Your pet's entire aquarium should be cleaned about every two to four weeks. To do this, first move your turtle to a temporary container. He should not stay in the tank while you clean it out.

Any lining materials should either be washed or replaced. Use a safe cleanser for the aquarium glass, rocks, and any other surfaces. Make sure to rinse everything well. There should be no traces of cleanser left when you put your turtle back in the tank.

Just like human fingernails, a turtle's claws never stop growing. His beak is always growing, too. Long claws can keep your turtle from walking properly. If his beak is overgrown, he may have difficulty chewing. Your pet's daily activities will wear down his claws and jaw a little, but this may not be enough. If your turtle's claws or beak get too long, take him to a veterinarian for trimming.

A turtle's **drinking water** should be changed **once a day**.

The biggest soft-shell turtles have shells **weighing** up to **309** pounds. (140 kilograms)

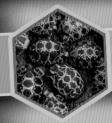

Some turtle species **cost** more than **$1,000** each.

Turtles may get sick if they are under stress. To avoid disturbing your turtle, keep him away from loud noises and do not tap on the glass of his tank.

# Healthy and Happy

When choosing a pet turtle, there are many factors to consider. Watch for signs that the turtle is healthy, such as clear eyes and a strong appetite. Her shell should be firm with few cracks.

Healthy turtles should also be able to breathe easily with a closed mouth. When you pick her up, the turtle should feel solid, not light. Check the folds of her skin for **parasites**. Water turtles should be able to swim easily below the surface.

As you and your pet become more familiar with each other, you will learn to observe her behavior. Soon, you will know which appearances are normal. Watch for any changes that could indicate illness. Does your pet have swollen or runny eyes? Has her appetite changed? Sores, swelling, unusual breathing sounds, or a softening shell are all symptoms that your turtle may be sick. Take her to a veterinarian if you notice any of these conditions.

One of the most common turtle illnesses is **fungus**. Fungus can grow in cracks or injuries on your turtle's shell. It will look like a cottony white film on the surface of your pet. Be very careful not to drop your turtle, since this may crack her shell.

Not all problems require a visit to the veterinarian. You can take care of simple issues at home. For instance, if your turtle flips over onto her shell, she may not be able to right herself. You can help by turning her over gently.

A turtle's feet are usually webbed, while a tortoise's feet are round and stumpy.

# Turtle Behavior

Not all turtles get along with other turtles. Before adding a second turtle to your tank, find out if your pet is aggressive or not. If he enjoys company, you may add another turtle to the tank. The more turtles you have, the larger their tank will need to be. To help prevent the spread of disease, you should **quarantine** the new turtle. Keep him separated from any other pets for the first four weeks. This will make sure he is not sick.

Most turtles do not like to be handled. Signs that your turtle does not enjoy being held may include kicking, biting, or tucking into his shell. It is usually best to hold your turtle only when necessary. You can pick him up carefully during cleaning times or to check his health.

If your pet is small, he can be held in the palm of your hand. Guard small turtles with your hand to prevent them from falling accidentally. Larger turtles can be lifted by placing one hand on either side of their body. To pick up a large turtle, put your thumbs on the carapace and your fingers under the plastron. Land turtles are more likely to enjoy physical contact than water turtles. Land turtles may like to have their shell or head stroked.

The Dr. Seuss National Memorial Sculpture Garden is in Springfield, Massachusetts. There are more than 30 statues, including one of King Yertle's throne.

# Turtle Tales

People have been fascinated by turtles for many years. Turtle characters appear in several books, television shows, and movies. In 1950, children's author Dr. Seuss wrote a book called *Yertle the Turtle and Other Stories*. In one story, King Yertle orders his kingdom to build him a throne from their shells. Hundreds of turtles pile on top of one another, with Yertle at the top. When one small turtle at the bottom of the pile decides he does not want to be part of the throne, it breaks.

Perhaps the most well-known turtles are the Teenage Mutant Ninja Turtles. These four turtles gained superhero powers when a chemical spilled on them. Now, they spend their time fighting villains in New York City. The Ninja Turtles have starred in comics, television shows, and movies since the late 1980s.

## The Tortoise and the Hare

One of the most classic stories featuring a turtle character is Aesop's fable "The Tortoise and the Hare." It is about a hare who brags of his speed. The hare thinks it is funny when the tortoise suggests that they race. When the race begins, the hare speeds past the tortoise. The tortoise follows slowly and steadily. Certain he will win the race, the hare decides he has time to take a nap. The tortoise passes the hare. When the hare wakes up, it is too late. The tortoise has already crossed the finish line. The moral of the story is that slow and steady wins the race.

# Pet Puzzlers

What do you know about turtles? If you can answer the following questions correctly, you may be ready to own a turtle.

**1** There are how many known species of turtles?

**2** The first turtles lived how many years ago?

**3** Red-eared sliders can live for how long?

**4** What are the two parts of a turtle's shell called?

**5** How long can the hatching process take?

**6** Why should you place a cover over your pet turtle's enclosure?

**7** Can a pet turtle overeat and get overweight?

**8** How often should a turtle's aquarium be cleaned?

**9** Do all turtles get along with other turtles?

**10** Are land turtles or water turtles more likely to enjoy physical contact?

# Turtle Tags

Before you buy your pet turtle, write down some turtle names you like. Some names may work better for a female turtle. Others may suit a male turtle. Here are just a few suggestions.

Myrtle

Scooter

Peanut

Tucker

Homer

Tommy

Sunny

Shelly

Peek-a-Boo

Speedy

# Key Words

**adapts:** becomes used to something

**basking:** lying under a heat source to warm oneself

**carnivorous:** meat eating

**fossils:** remains of ancient animals and plants from long ago found in rocks

**fungus:** a plantlike organism that appears as fuzz on the skin

**hibernate:** to spend a period of time in a sleeplike state

**incubator:** a container used to keep eggs warm so that they will hatch

**keratin:** the strong substance that makes a turtle's shell hard; the same substance found in human fingernails

**parasites:** organisms that live on or in other living beings

**predators:** animals that hunt and kill other animals for food

**quarantine:** temporary separation from others

**scutes:** bony plates on a turtle's shell

**supplements:** things that are added to something to make it better

**veterinarian:** animal doctor

# Index

# Get the best of both worlds.

AV2 bridges the gap between print and digital.

The expandable resources toolbar enables quick access to content including **videos**, **audio**, **activities**, **weblinks**, **slideshows**, **quizzes**, and **key words**.

**Animated videos** make static images come alive.

Resource icons on each page help readers to further **explore key concepts**.

Published by AV2
350 5th Avenue, 59th Floor
New York, NY 10118
Website: www.av2books.com

Library of Congress Cataloging-in-Publication Data

Names: Hamilton, Lynn, 1964- author. | Gillespie, Katie, author.
Title: Turtle / Lynn Hamilton and Katie Gillespie.
Description: New York, NY : AV2 by Weigl, [2020] | Series: Pets we love | Includes index. | Audience: Grades 4-6 |
Identifiers: LCCN 2019047985 (print) | LCCN 2019047986 (ebook) | ISBN 9781791119287 (library binding) | ISBN 9781791119294 (paperback) | ISBN 9781791119300 (ebook other) | ISBN 9781791119317 (ebook other)
Subjects: LCSH: Turtles as pets--Juvenile literature.
Classification: LCC SF459.T8 H3423 2020 (print) | LCC SF459.T8 (ebook) | DDC 639.3/92--dc23

LC record available at https://lccn.loc.gov/2019047985
LC ebook record available at https://lccn.loc.gov/2019047986

Printed in Guangzhou, China
1 2 3 4 5 6 7 8 9 0 24 23 22 21 20

022020
101319

Project Coordinator Sara Cucini
Art Director Terry Paulhus

Photo Credits
Every reasonable effort has been made to trace ownership and to obtain permission to reprint copyright material. The publishers would be pleased to have any errors or omissions brought to their attention so that they may be corrected in subsequent printings. AV2 acknowledges Getty Images, Alamy, and Shutterstock as its primary photo suppliers for this title.

om